Explorin

Fascinating Facts for Young Learners.

By Author Jamie Pedrazzoli

ISBN: 9798392316151

This book is dedicated to my beautiful daughters.

The names in this book are used fictitiously and any resemblance of persons is coincidental. The facts in this book are based on information provided to the author.

I attempted to put the sound of foreign words in parenthesis to help you pronounce them easier.

Please remember that I speak English so I am attempting to help others pronounce the words by the way I hear them.

مـرحبًـا

(Mer-hah-bahn) or Hello.
My name is Ishmael (ees-my-ell). I
live in the Hashemite Kingdom of
Jordan located in Southwest Asia.

I am a Bedouin (Bed-ah-wee-in). Our name means 'Desert People.' I live a nomadic lifestyle, which means I travel a lot.

My family usually moves from one water source to another. Most Bedouins are animal herders who migrate into the desert during the rainy winter season and move back toward the cultivated land in the dry summer months.

My family herds sheep and goats.

We live in tents called Byoot Shars (bah-yoot sharz). My house is made of hair!

That's right you heard me correctly. My house is a tent made of hair from goats and camels.

We live in tents so that we can put up and take down our homes quickly.

Inside my home, there is an area for men called the shig, and an area for the woman called the mahram. The divider is called the saha. Guests always enter on the men's side.

We also have rugs inside and mattresses that are stuffed with wool. We use mattresses to sleep and sit.

The rugs are made on a loom and dyed colors made from vegetable dyes. They are called b'saat (bah-saat)

Bedouins are known for making silver jewelry.

We have no electricity.

We use camels for transportation. As a cultural tradition, camel races are held during celebratory occasions, such as weddings or religious festivals.

Have you ever seen a camel?

We usually eat dates milk, yogurt, meat, and cheese from animals.

Mansaf is a Bedouin dish that is served on special occasions. It is made from lamb, drizzled with a yogurt sauce, and served with rice, almonds, and pine nuts.

For entertainment, we watch a Sahjeh or dance that tells a story from the past.

I want to tell you more facts about my country.

The Hashemite Kingdom of Jordan is almost landlocked and only has 6 miles or 26 kilometers of coastline on the Gulf of Aqaba.

The East and South coasts of Jordan are dominated by the Syrian Desert also known as the North Arabian Desert. It is covered in volcanic lava, basalt, and sand. This area is unfit for agriculture.

The Southern area consists of rock formations that stick out above ground made up of sandstone and granite.

East of the Jordan River is the uplands. They are 2,000 to 3,000 feet in elevation and are home to most of the population.

There are valleys, streams, and riverbeds that crisscross the uplands.

This is me in front of the Jordan River.

The Jordan Valley forms part of the Great Rift Valley which extends into Africa. It has steep slopes.

The Dead Sea is in the central area of the Great Rift Valley. North of the Dead Sea is the most fertile land.

South of the Dead Sea is the Wadi al-Arabah which is believed to contain minerals and this is part of the border that separates Israel from Jordan.

Here is a photo of me and my sister, Naya in the Great Rift Valley.

Both the Eastern and Southern areas of Jordan have desert climates. The Capital city of Amman has a temperature of 79 degrees Fahrenheit or 26 Degrees Celsius in the summer.

In the winter the temperature is 46 degrees Fahrenheit or 8 degrees Celsius.

The desert regions can reach 120 degrees Fahrenheit or 49 degrees Celsius.

Did you know that the desert regions receive less than 4 inches or 10 centimeters of rain per year?

The Al Azraq Oasis is 68 miles or 110 kilometers from the capital city of Amman. This oasis is the only source of water in Jordan's entire eastern desert!

The desert that surrounds the oasis consists of old castles. Qasr al-Azraq is one of the desert castles.

There is a Wetland Nature Reserve in Azraq. A boardwalk is being built over the oasis so you can walk along and enjoy the wildlife.

What kind of wildlife is in Jordan?

Can you guess some of the animals that can be found here?

In the Oasis you can find the flamingo bird and many others, such as the Sinai Rose finch. This is the National Bird of Jordan.

There are water buffalo that like to come to the Oasis of Azraq to cool down in the hot summers.

The endangered Nubian Ibex, Syrian wolf, gazelle, wildcat, fox, mongoose, roe deer, and striped hyena are a few of the animals found in Jordan.

There is also the Imperial Eagle, Kestrel (a type of falcon), and Griffon Vulture.

The Dana Reserve holds over 698 plant species and about 555 animal species!

The Shaumari Reserve holds the national animal of Jordan, the Arabian Oryx. This beautiful animal is endangered and there are only about 200 that roam free here.

Many lizards and snakes can be found in Jordan, including the dangerous Palestinian viper and the Puff Adder.

There are also poisonous scorpions found in desert areas.

There is only one seaport in Jordan and that is in Aqaba. It is a thriving tourist attraction because it holds rare marine life and coral.

People come here to swim, snorkel, dive, picnic, and go to the beach.

Starfish, sea cucumber, crab, shrimp, urchin, fish, black tip sharks, hammerhead sharks, and whale sharks can be found in these waters.

The Black Iris is the National Flower.

98% of the people in Jordan are Arab. The three main groups are the Transjordan, Palestinian Arabs, and the Bedouins. The 2% remaining is made up of other ethnic groups.

The official language in my country is Arabic. English is also widely spoken here.

Spoken Arabic is called 'Aami.'
Written Arabic is called, 'Fusha.'

The Arabic Script is written and read from right to left and consists of 28 letters.

Here are some phrases in the Arabic Language.

كيف حالك

Kayf Haluk (kay-fuh-hah-loo-kah) How are you?

بخير، شكرا لك

bikhayrin, shukran lak (meh-hi-rin-shook-ran-lah-kah) Fine, thank you.

مساء الخير

masa' alkhayr (mah-sah-el-hi-ree) Good Afternoon.

اسمي هو

asmi hu (ess-me-who-uh) My name is ..

مع السلامة

mae alsalama (mah-ah-sah-lahm-ah) Goodbye.

مـرحبًـا

(Mer-hah-bahn) or Hello.
My name is Malik (mah-leek). I live
in Aqaba.

Aqaba is a Jordanian port city. It
is located on the Red Sea's Gulf of
Aqaba.

What is there to do where I live?

Many people visit the Aqaba bird observatory, the Aqaba Water Park, the Ayla Oasis, the Berenice Beach Club, the Sharif Hussain Mosque, the Wadi Rum protected area, the Aqaba Museum, and the Aqaba Fort.

Many people like to snorkel and dive here as well.

This is me at the Aqaba Water Park. Does this place look fun to you?

The population estimate of Jordan in 2021 was 11.15 million.

The currency we use here is the Jordan Dinar. 0.71 JOD equals about $1 US dollar.

The major religions here are Islam and Christianity. About 92 % of the people practice Islam; 6 % practice Christianity.

In the Islam faith, we believe in one God, Allah. We believe that Muhammad was his prophet.

We pray 5 times a day, donate money to the poor, and journey on a pilgrimage to the Holy City of Mecca in Saudi Arabia once in our lifetime.

Our place of worship is called a Mosque. There are separate areas for men and women.

Here is a photo of me and my brother, Ahmed in front of the Aqaba Mosque.

This is the flag of Jordan. It has horizontal bands of black, white, and green.

This represents the Abbasid, Umayyad, and Fatimid dynasties. The red triangle stands for the great Arab revolt of 1916 and the Hashemite dynasty.

The seven-pointed white star in the red triangle's center symbolizes the Holy Qur'an's first seven verses. The seven points represent faith in one God, humanity, national spirit, humility, social justice, virtue, and aspiration.

Now I will tell you about the history of Jordan.

In the 13th century in the North was the Ammon, in the center was the Moab, and in the South, various kingdoms emerged.

1000 BC King David controlled most of the area.

In the 9th century, the Assyrians conquered the Eastern area. At the fall of the Assyrian Empire, the Babylonian Empire rose.

In 539 B.C. Cyrus II, the Persians ended Babylonian rule.

In 106 A.D. the Kingdom became Arabia Petraea under Roman rule.

In 636 A.D. the Arab Muslims invaded the lands bringing the Islam religion with them.

In 1517 the Ottoman Turks made this area become part of the Ottoman Empire.

The British revolt helped cause the downfall of this empire around WWI.

Following WWI, the area which is present-day Israel and Jordan was the British Mandate of Palestine.

In 1947, the newly formed United Nations accepted the idea to partition Palestine into a zone for the Jews (Israel) and a zone for the Arabs (Palestine). With this United Nations proposal, the British withdrew from the region on May 14th, 1948. The name changed to the Hashemite Kingdom of Jordan in 1949.

In 1948 Jordan and its Arab neighbors attacked Israel sparking the Arab-Israeli War.

In 1967 a six-day war broke out because of the tensions formed between the Arab and Israeli.

Peace was soon restored.

In 1991 Jordan became involved in the American-Israeli Peace initiatives and three years later a peace treaty was signed between Israel and Jordan.

This ended 46 years of war!

What type of Government does Jordan have?

The Government in Jordan today is a Constitutional Monarchy. It has legislative, executive, and Judicial branches.

The King appoints a Prime Minister.
The King exercises his executive
authority through the Prime Minister
and cabinet.

Thank you for listening to me give
you some information on my country.

مع السلامة

mae alsalama (mah-ah-sah-lahm-ah)
Goodbye.

مـرحبًـا

(Mer-hah-bahn) or Hello.
My name is Salma (sahl-mah).

I live in the Capital city of Amman.
It is a very big city full of many
buildings and busy streets. It is
also called the safest city in the
Middle East.

What is there to do where I live?

Many people like to visit the Roman Theater, the Roman temple of Hercules, the Amman Citadel National Historic Site, the Jordan National Gallery of Fine Arts, the Royal Tank Museum, and the Children's Museum.

Family life is very important to the people of Jordan. Many relatives live in the same neighborhood.

The father is usually the decision maker. The mother stays home to look after the children. Many families have three or four children.

Children are cherished and the elderly are well respected.

Here is a photo of me with my brothers and sister.

Families usually have picnics; tell stories, dance, and play games such as Chess, Backgammon, and Shutterunge (Shoe-ter-unj) a game similar to the American game of Checkers.

At school, we sometimes play Hajli (Haj-lee) which is like hopscotch. We also play Ghalool (gha-lool) or marbles.

87% of people in my country can read. Government schools provide free education from elementary to high school.

Ages six to fifteen attend school. Education beyond tenth grade is optional.

The Secondary school specializes in vocational courses and ends with an exam, or tawjihi (toe-jee-hee). If you pass the tawjihi you can go to Community College.

The Ministry of Education supervises schools. We learn Arabic, math, physics, chemistry, biology, social science, geography, religion, history, and English.

Do you take some of the same classes at your school?

**

What is it like to be a woman in Jordan?

According to Jordan's constitution, men and women are equal. Both can run for office and work.

In 1989 women got to vote for the first time.

In 1999 Rima Khalaf was the first Deputy Prime Minister.

Today half of the students are female and only about 14% of women in Jordan can't read.

Women in Jordan are not required to wear hijabs but many choose to. The hijab is a head covering worn by women.

Jordanian women dress very fashionably in urban parts of the country.

In small villages or conservative areas, many women wear a long coat called a jilbab(jee-bahb), which covers any hint of their figure.

At a resort, anything goes, but at a public beach, you may want to choose a modest swimsuit if you choose to visit.

So, what do we eat in Jordan?

I love to eat bananas, figs, dates, apricots, grapes, yogurt, herbs, spices, and nuts.

Many people eat meats like lamb and chicken, grains, cheese, and vegetables.

Khubez (koh-biz) is a type of bread that is eaten with every meal. It is a round, flatbread.

I love hummus. Have you tried it? It is a paste made from chickpeas.

Tabbouleh is a salad of chopped parsley, tomatoes, and onion.

Baba Ghanoush (bah-bah gahn-nooj) is a dip made of smoked eggplant and sesame paste.

For dessert, I like to eat pastries with nut and cheese filling covered in sweet syrup.

I also like milk and rice pudding and ice cream.

We do not eat pork and we only eat with our right hands.

The left hand is considered unclean.

The most popular drink in my country is coffee. I serve it to guests when they enter and again when they leave. We serve coffee in a long-handled copper coffee pot.

It is an insult to refuse coffee because it is considered a symbol of hospitality and goodwill.

Here is my mother, Layan drinking coffee.

I want to tell you about some amazing places in my country.

I will start by talking about the Dead Sea.

Have you heard of it?

We call it al-bahr al-mayyit (ahl-bahr-ahl-mah-yeet). It is the lowest body of water on Earth. It is 1,312 feet or 400 meters below sea level.

It is land-locked and is 50 miles or 80 kilometers in length and 11 miles or 18 kilometers wide. This Sea is located between Israel and Jordan.

The Dead Sea is a very popular tourist attraction. The minerals in the water are said to have medical and beautification uses. There are said to be 21 different minerals in this Sea.

This Sea is 7 times saltier than the ocean. There is no plant or animal life in it, only bacteria can survive.

There is also mineral-rich mud around the Sea.

Speaking of the Dead Sea, have you heard of the Dead Sea Scrolls?

The Dead Sea Scrolls were found in the Judean Desert. This is one of the most important archaeological discoveries ever!

North of the Capital City is Jerash. This is a beautifully preserved Roman city that formed part of a Decapolis.

A Decapolis means 10 cities in the Greek language.

Madaba is a famous city in West Jordan because of its mosaics.

Mosaics are made of small pieces of glass, marble, or stone and are used to decorate floors.

In Madaba, there is a mosaic map which is known as the oldest map in the region. It was made in A.D. 560. It is 72 feet or 22 meters by 23 feet or 7 meters in size. Parts of this mosaic have been destroyed by age but there are still 150 Greek inscriptions on it that are still legible.

Petra is my favorite place to visit! Its name means, 'Rock.' This city was built in ancient times and is in Southwest Jordan.

Swiss Explorer, Johann Ludwig located this hidden city in 1812.

The entrance is carved out of rock from the side of a mountain. It is 131 feet or 40 meters high.

**

Weddings are a major event here. Most men wait until they are in their 30s to marry because they usually cannot afford to marry sooner.

Weddings are a costly event in Jordan, second to buying a house.

Most couples meet through family interactions. The bride receives a Mahr, or dowry from the groom. The bride can spend or save the dowry however she chooses. The amount of Mahr depends on the family's circumstances.

What else do we celebrate in Jordan?

We celebrate Ramadan, which is the Islamic month of fasting. We do not eat, drink, or smoke during daylight hours.

Eid al Fitr is a three-day festival that celebrates the end of Ramadan. We usually pray at a mosque and then visit friends.

Eid al Adha is the feast of the sacrifice celebrated in the last month of the year, following the Muslim pilgrimage to Mecca, also called the hajj. This festival commemorates Abraham's willingness to sacrifice his only son to God.

We also celebrate Independence Day, King Abdullah II's ascent to the throne, King Abdullah's birthday, and some people celebrate Christmas.

**

What kind of sports do we have in Jordan?

Horse racing and equestrian events are very popular.

Many girls practice gymnastics.

Some children take martial arts.

Soccer(football) is probably the most popular sport in Jordan.

Here is my brother Zaid playing soccer.

Car rallying is a popular sport. We have a Jordan International Car Rally once per year that attracts many tourists from around the world. There are many international competitors.

Wadi Rum is a sport of challenging rock climbing that is practiced in South Jordan.

Thank you for listening to me speak about my wonderful country. I hope you learned many things.

THE END.

Other books in this series include:

Exploring Romania

Exploring Ireland

Exploring Costa Rica

Exploring New Zealand

Exploring Germany

Exploring Zambia

Exploring Mexico

Exploring Japan

Exploring the Philippines

Exploring India

Exploring South Africa

Other books in the Around the World Series include:

Denmark

India

Romania

Costa Rica

Vietnam

Zambia

Germany

Jordan

The Philippines

Ireland

Mexico

Japan

South Africa

Ukraine

New Zealand

Please support me as an author by checking out my other books available under Jamie Bach. My books can be purchased online at most online bookstores.

<u>**For kids and young adults**</u>

Tongue-twisting alphabet fun with Koby Jack and Bogart

Counting shapes and color fun with Koby Jack and Bogart

My Jungle Adventure in Costa Rica

Jess the Fox (also in Spanish) Jess el Zorro

Florida girls

Florida girls 2

Let's learn sight words Kindergarten

For Adults or Teens

Aleida Orphan no more a Cinderella story with a twist

Words of encouragement and how to cope with what life brings you

Untrusting Eyes

School for the Enchanted

About the Author

Jamie Pedrazzoli (Jamie Bach) grew up in Vero Beach Florida where she spent time taking art classes in high school with the Center for the Arts Museum. She always enjoyed reading and writing.

She has three daughters that help inspire her to write.

"I'm so glad I can share my books with the world; I hope everyone enjoys reading them".

Check out her website and other links to social media.

Author site on Facebook

https://www.facebook.com/jamiebachauthorchildrensbooks

Author sites

http://authorjamiebach.weebly.com

http://zolibooks.weebly.com

Twitter

https://twitter.com/jamiebach421

Adventure Blog

http://theadventuresofkobyjackandbogart.weebly.com

Instagram

https://www.instagram.com/jamiepedrazzoliauthor

http://www.instagram.com/jamiebach421author

Remember if you wish to contact this author an email address is provided. Do not call her or her parents' home. This is an invasion of privacy and is not appreciated. If it is of urgent importance EMAIL is the best way.

That email is pedrazzolij@yahoo.com

Have an adult help you cut out the collectible bookmark to use while reading this book.

Made in the USA
Las Vegas, NV
23 October 2024

10410189R00038